50 United Kingdom Shake Recipes for Home

By: Kelly Johnson

Table of Contents

- Earl Grey Tea Shake
- Sticky Toffee Pudding Shake
- Banoffee Pie Shake
- British Berry Crumble Shake
- Yorkshire Pudding Shake
- Treacle Tart Shake
- Spotted Dick Shake
- Rhubarb and Custard Shake
- Apple Crumble Shake
- Custard Cream Shake
- Blackcurrant Cordial Shake
- Lemon Drizzle Cake Shake
- Gingerbread Biscuit Shake
- Victoria Sponge Shake
- Chocolate Digestive Shake
- Classic British Scone Shake
- Minced Pie Shake
- Bread and Butter Pudding Shake
- Pimm's Summer Shake
- Cherry Bakewell Shake
- Jelly and Ice Cream Shake
- Toad in the Hole Shake
- Plum Pudding Shake
- English Breakfast Tea Shake
- Fruit and Nut Bar Shake
- Bakewell Tart Shake
- Mince Pie Shake
- Scone and Clotted Cream Shake
- Welsh Cakes Shake
- Rhubarb Fool Shake
- Chocolate and Orange Jaffa Cake Shake
- Summer Fruits Eton Mess Shake

- Spicy Apple and Cinnamon Shake
- Raspberry Ripple Shake
- Chocolate Mint Aero Shake
- Lemon Curd Shake
- Caramel Shortbread Shake
- Fruity Jam Roly-Poly Shake
- Nutella and Banana British Classic Shake
- Oat Biscuit Shake
- Plum and Almond Bake Shake
- Lemon and Poppy Seed Shake
- Victoria Sponge with Strawberry Shake
- Pecan Pie Shake
- Blackberry and Apple Crumble Shake
- Rhubarb and Ginger Shake
- Chocolate Marshmallow Shake
- Peach Melba Shake
- Traditional English Trifle Shake
- Sticky Date and Walnut Shake

Earl Grey Tea Shake

Ingredients:

- 1 cup milk (dairy or non-dairy, such as almond or oat milk)
- 1/2 cup Greek yogurt (plain or vanilla)
- 1 tablespoon loose Earl Grey tea leaves or 1 Earl Grey tea bag
- 1 tablespoon honey or maple syrup (adjust to taste)
- 1/4 teaspoon vanilla extract
- 1/4 teaspoon ground cardamom (optional, for extra flavor)
- Ice cubes (as needed)
- Optional: 1 scoop vanilla protein powder (for added protein)

Instructions:

1. **Brew Tea:** If using loose tea leaves, steep them in 1/2 cup hot water for about 3-5 minutes, then strain. If using a tea bag, steep it in 1/2 cup hot water for the same amount of time. Allow the tea to cool slightly.
2. **Blend Ingredients:** In a blender, combine the brewed tea, milk, Greek yogurt, honey or maple syrup, and vanilla extract. If using, add ground cardamom and/or protein powder.
3. **Add Ice:** Add a handful of ice cubes for a thicker, colder shake.
4. **Blend:** Blend on high until smooth and creamy. If the shake is too thick, add more milk to achieve your desired consistency.
5. **Taste and Adjust:** Taste the shake and adjust sweetness or flavor if needed by adding more honey or vanilla extract.
6. **Serve:** Pour the shake into a glass and enjoy immediately.

Enjoy your Earl Grey Tea Shake! It's a creamy, elegant treat with the aromatic flavors of Earl Grey tea, perfect for a sophisticated twist on a classic shake.

Sticky Toffee Pudding Shake

Ingredients:

- 1 cup milk (dairy or non-dairy, such as almond or oat milk)
- 1/2 cup vanilla ice cream (or dairy-free ice cream)
- 1/2 cup Greek yogurt (plain or vanilla)
- 1/4 cup dates (pitted and chopped)
- 2 tablespoons toffee sauce (store-bought or homemade)
- 1/4 teaspoon ground cinnamon
- 1/4 teaspoon vanilla extract
- Ice cubes (as needed)
- Optional: Whipped cream and extra toffee sauce (for garnish)

Instructions:

1. **Prepare Dates:** If using dried dates, soak them in warm water for about 10 minutes to soften. Drain and chop them before use.
2. **Blend Ingredients:** In a blender, combine the milk, vanilla ice cream, Greek yogurt, chopped dates, toffee sauce, ground cinnamon, and vanilla extract.
3. **Add Ice:** Add a handful of ice cubes for a thicker, colder shake.
4. **Blend:** Blend on high until smooth and creamy. If the shake is too thick, add more milk to achieve your desired consistency.
5. **Taste and Adjust:** Taste the shake and adjust sweetness or flavor if needed by adding more toffee sauce.
6. **Serve:** Pour the shake into a glass. Optionally, top with whipped cream and drizzle with extra toffee sauce.

Enjoy your Sticky Toffee Pudding Shake! It's a decadent and creamy treat that brings together the comforting flavors of sticky toffee pudding in a deliciously refreshing shake.

Banoffee Pie Shake

Ingredients:

- 1 large banana (peeled and sliced)
- 1/2 cup vanilla ice cream (or dairy-free ice cream)
- 1/2 cup milk (dairy or non-dairy, such as almond or oat milk)
- 2 tablespoons toffee sauce (store-bought or homemade)
- 1/2 cup Greek yogurt (plain or vanilla)
- 1 tablespoon instant coffee granules (dissolved in 1 tablespoon hot water)
- 1/4 teaspoon vanilla extract
- Ice cubes (as needed)
- Optional: Crumbled digestive biscuits or graham crackers (for garnish)

Instructions:

1. **Prepare Coffee:** Dissolve the instant coffee granules in hot water and let it cool slightly.
2. **Blend Ingredients:** In a blender, combine the banana, vanilla ice cream, milk, toffee sauce, Greek yogurt, dissolved coffee, and vanilla extract.
3. **Add Ice:** Add a handful of ice cubes for a thicker, colder shake.
4. **Blend:** Blend on high until smooth and creamy. If the shake is too thick, add more milk to achieve your desired consistency.
5. **Taste and Adjust:** Taste the shake and adjust sweetness or coffee flavor if needed by adding more toffee sauce or coffee.
6. **Serve:** Pour the shake into a glass. Optionally, garnish with crumbled digestive biscuits or graham crackers for a bit of crunch and extra flavor.

Enjoy your Banoffee Pie Shake! It's a creamy and indulgent shake that perfectly blends the flavors of banana, toffee, and a touch of coffee, bringing the beloved banoffee pie into a refreshing drink form.

British Berry Crumble Shake

Ingredients:

- 1 cup mixed berries (fresh or frozen; strawberries, raspberries, and blueberries work well)
- 1/2 cup vanilla ice cream (or dairy-free ice cream)
- 1/2 cup Greek yogurt (plain or vanilla)
- 1/2 cup milk (dairy or non-dairy, such as almond or oat milk)
- 1/4 cup granola or oat crumble (for a crumble texture)
- 1 tablespoon honey or maple syrup (adjust to taste)
- 1/4 teaspoon vanilla extract
- Ice cubes (as needed)
- Optional: Extra granola or fresh berries (for garnish)

Instructions:

1. **Blend Ingredients:** In a blender, combine the mixed berries, vanilla ice cream, Greek yogurt, milk, granola or oat crumble, honey or maple syrup, and vanilla extract.
2. **Add Ice:** Add a handful of ice cubes for a thicker, colder shake.
3. **Blend:** Blend on high until smooth and creamy. If the shake is too thick, add more milk to reach your desired consistency.
4. **Taste and Adjust:** Taste the shake and adjust sweetness if needed by adding more honey or maple syrup.
5. **Serve:** Pour the shake into a glass. Optionally, garnish with extra granola or fresh berries for added texture and flavor.

Enjoy your British Berry Crumble Shake! It's a deliciously creamy treat that combines the fruity flavors of mixed berries with the comforting crunch of a crumble, making for a delightful and refreshing shake.

Yorkshire Pudding Shake

Ingredients:

- 1 cup milk (dairy or non-dairy, such as almond or oat milk)
- 1/2 cup vanilla ice cream (or dairy-free ice cream)
- 1/2 cup Greek yogurt (plain or vanilla)
- 1/4 cup cooked Yorkshire pudding (chopped into small pieces; you can use store-bought or homemade)
- 1 tablespoon maple syrup or honey (adjust to taste)
- 1/4 teaspoon vanilla extract
- 1/4 teaspoon ground cinnamon (optional, for a touch of warmth)
- Ice cubes (as needed)
- Optional: Whipped cream and a sprinkle of powdered sugar or additional cinnamon (for garnish)

Instructions:

1. **Prepare Yorkshire Pudding:** If using store-bought Yorkshire pudding, chop it into small pieces. If homemade, allow it to cool slightly and then chop.
2. **Blend Ingredients:** In a blender, combine the milk, vanilla ice cream, Greek yogurt, chopped Yorkshire pudding, maple syrup or honey, vanilla extract, and ground cinnamon if using.
3. **Add Ice:** Add a handful of ice cubes for a thicker, colder shake.
4. **Blend:** Blend on high until smooth and creamy. If the shake is too thick, add more milk to achieve your desired consistency.
5. **Taste and Adjust:** Taste the shake and adjust sweetness or spice if needed by adding more maple syrup or cinnamon.
6. **Serve:** Pour the shake into a glass. Optionally, top with whipped cream and a sprinkle of powdered sugar or additional cinnamon for extra indulgence.

Enjoy your Yorkshire Pudding Shake! It's a creative and creamy shake that incorporates the comforting flavors of Yorkshire pudding, offering a unique and nostalgic twist on a classic dessert.

Treacle Tart Shake

Ingredients:

- 1 cup milk (dairy or non-dairy, such as almond or oat milk)
- 1/2 cup vanilla ice cream (or dairy-free ice cream)
- 1/2 cup Greek yogurt (plain or vanilla)
- 1/4 cup golden syrup or dark treacle (for that signature treacle flavor)
- 1/4 cup crushed digestive biscuits or graham crackers (for a bit of crust texture)
- 1/4 teaspoon ground ginger (optional, for extra warmth)
- 1/4 teaspoon vanilla extract
- Ice cubes (as needed)
- Optional: Whipped cream and extra crushed biscuits (for garnish)

Instructions:

1. **Blend Ingredients:** In a blender, combine the milk, vanilla ice cream, Greek yogurt, golden syrup or dark treacle, crushed digestive biscuits or graham crackers, ground ginger (if using), and vanilla extract.
2. **Add Ice:** Add a handful of ice cubes for a thicker, colder shake.
3. **Blend:** Blend on high until smooth and creamy. If the shake is too thick, add more milk to reach your desired consistency.
4. **Taste and Adjust:** Taste the shake and adjust sweetness if needed by adding more golden syrup or treacle.
5. **Serve:** Pour the shake into a glass. Optionally, top with whipped cream and a sprinkle of extra crushed biscuits for added texture and indulgence.

Enjoy your Treacle Tart Shake! It's a rich and creamy treat that beautifully blends the sweet, sticky essence of treacle tart with the smooth texture of a milkshake, making for a delightful and nostalgic dessert experience.

Spotted Dick Shake

Ingredients:

- 1 cup milk (dairy or non-dairy, such as almond or oat milk)
- 1/2 cup vanilla ice cream (or dairy-free ice cream)
- 1/2 cup Greek yogurt (plain or vanilla)
- 1/4 cup dried currants or raisins (for the "spots")
- 2 tablespoons sponge cake or crumbled digestive biscuits (to mimic the pudding texture)
- 2 tablespoons golden syrup or honey (for sweetness)
- 1/4 teaspoon ground cinnamon (optional, for extra warmth)
- 1/4 teaspoon vanilla extract
- Ice cubes (as needed)
- Optional: Whipped cream and extra currants or raisins (for garnish)

Instructions:

1. **Soften Currants:** If the dried currants or raisins are very dry, soak them in a little warm water for about 10 minutes to soften, then drain.
2. **Blend Ingredients:** In a blender, combine the milk, vanilla ice cream, Greek yogurt, softened currants or raisins, crumbled sponge cake or digestive biscuits, golden syrup or honey, ground cinnamon (if using), and vanilla extract.
3. **Add Ice:** Add a handful of ice cubes for a thicker, colder shake.
4. **Blend:** Blend on high until smooth and creamy. If the shake is too thick, add more milk to achieve your desired consistency.
5. **Taste and Adjust:** Taste the shake and adjust sweetness if needed by adding more golden syrup or honey.
6. **Serve:** Pour the shake into a glass. Optionally, top with whipped cream and a sprinkle of extra currants or raisins for added texture and indulgence.

Enjoy your Spotted Dick Shake! It's a fun and creamy take on a classic British dessert, combining the sweet and comforting flavors of spotted dick with the refreshing texture of a milkshake.

Rhubarb and Custard Shake

Ingredients:

- 1 cup milk (dairy or non-dairy, such as almond or oat milk)
- 1/2 cup vanilla ice cream (or dairy-free ice cream)
- 1/2 cup Greek yogurt (plain or vanilla)
- 1/2 cup cooked rhubarb (sweetened to taste, cooled)
- 2 tablespoons custard powder (or 1/2 cup pre-made custard, if preferred)
- 1-2 tablespoons honey or maple syrup (adjust to taste)
- 1/4 teaspoon vanilla extract
- Ice cubes (as needed)
- Optional: Crumbled shortbread or digestive biscuits (for garnish)

Instructions:

1. **Prepare Rhubarb:** Cook rhubarb in a small pan with a little water and sugar (or honey) until tender, about 10 minutes. Let it cool before using. You can also use store-bought rhubarb compote if preferred.
2. **Blend Ingredients:** In a blender, combine the milk, vanilla ice cream, Greek yogurt, cooked rhubarb, custard powder (or pre-made custard), honey or maple syrup, and vanilla extract.
3. **Add Ice:** Add a handful of ice cubes for a thicker, colder shake.
4. **Blend:** Blend on high until smooth and creamy. If the shake is too thick, add more milk to reach your desired consistency.
5. **Taste and Adjust:** Taste the shake and adjust sweetness if needed by adding more honey or maple syrup.
6. **Serve:** Pour the shake into a glass. Optionally, garnish with crumbled shortbread or digestive biscuits for added texture and a touch of extra flavor.

Enjoy your Rhubarb and Custard Shake! It's a creamy and nostalgic treat that combines the tartness of rhubarb with the comforting sweetness of custard, making for a delightful and refreshing shake.

Apple Crumble Shake

Ingredients:

- 1 cup milk (dairy or non-dairy, such as almond or oat milk)
- 1/2 cup vanilla ice cream (or dairy-free ice cream)
- 1/2 cup Greek yogurt (plain or vanilla)
- 1 cup cooked and cooled apple filling (like from an apple pie or homemade apple compote)
- 1/4 cup crumbled crumble topping or granola (for texture)
- 1 tablespoon maple syrup or honey (adjust to taste)
- 1/2 teaspoon ground cinnamon
- 1/4 teaspoon vanilla extract
- Ice cubes (as needed)
- Optional: Whipped cream and extra crumble topping or apple slices (for garnish)

Instructions:

1. **Prepare Apple Filling:** If using fresh apples, peel, core, and chop them. Cook the apples in a pan with a little water, sugar, and cinnamon until tender, about 10 minutes. Let them cool before using. Alternatively, you can use pre-made apple compote or apple pie filling.
2. **Blend Ingredients:** In a blender, combine the milk, vanilla ice cream, Greek yogurt, apple filling, crumbled crumble topping or granola, maple syrup or honey, ground cinnamon, and vanilla extract.
3. **Add Ice:** Add a handful of ice cubes for a thicker, colder shake.
4. **Blend:** Blend on high until smooth and creamy. If the shake is too thick, add more milk to reach your desired consistency.
5. **Taste and Adjust:** Taste the shake and adjust sweetness or spice if needed by adding more maple syrup or cinnamon.
6. **Serve:** Pour the shake into a glass. Optionally, top with whipped cream and a sprinkle of extra crumble topping or a few apple slices for extra indulgence.

Enjoy your Apple Crumble Shake! It's a deliciously creamy treat that combines the flavors of sweet apples, cinnamon, and a crunchy crumble topping, making for a comforting and refreshing shake.

Custard Cream Shake

Ingredients:

- 1 cup milk (dairy or non-dairy, such as almond or oat milk)
- 1/2 cup vanilla ice cream (or dairy-free ice cream)
- 1/2 cup Greek yogurt (plain or vanilla)
- 4-6 Custard Cream biscuits (crushed)
- 1 tablespoon custard powder (or 1/4 cup pre-made custard, if preferred)
- 1 tablespoon honey or maple syrup (adjust to taste)
- 1/4 teaspoon vanilla extract
- Ice cubes (as needed)
- Optional: Whipped cream and extra crushed Custard Cream biscuits (for garnish)

Instructions:

1. **Crush Biscuits:** Crush the Custard Cream biscuits into small pieces. You can do this using a food processor or by placing them in a sealed bag and crushing them with a rolling pin.
2. **Blend Ingredients:** In a blender, combine the milk, vanilla ice cream, Greek yogurt, crushed Custard Cream biscuits, custard powder (or pre-made custard), honey or maple syrup, and vanilla extract.
3. **Add Ice:** Add a handful of ice cubes for a thicker, colder shake.
4. **Blend:** Blend on high until smooth and creamy. If the shake is too thick, add more milk to achieve your desired consistency.
5. **Taste and Adjust:** Taste the shake and adjust sweetness if needed by adding more honey or maple syrup.
6. **Serve:** Pour the shake into a glass. Optionally, top with whipped cream and a sprinkle of extra crushed Custard Cream biscuits for added texture and indulgence.

Enjoy your Custard Cream Shake! It's a creamy, nostalgic treat that perfectly blends the flavors of custard and classic Custard Cream biscuits, making for a deliciously indulgent milkshake.

Blackcurrant Cordial Shake

Ingredients:

- 1 cup milk (dairy or non-dairy, such as almond or oat milk)
- 1/2 cup vanilla ice cream (or dairy-free ice cream)
- 1/2 cup Greek yogurt (plain or vanilla)
- 1/4 cup blackcurrant cordial (adjust to taste)
- 1/4 cup frozen blackcurrants or mixed berries (optional, for extra fruitiness)
- 1 tablespoon honey or maple syrup (adjust to taste)
- 1/4 teaspoon vanilla extract
- Ice cubes (as needed)
- Optional: Fresh mint leaves or extra blackcurrants (for garnish)

Instructions:

1. **Blend Ingredients:** In a blender, combine the milk, vanilla ice cream, Greek yogurt, blackcurrant cordial, and frozen blackcurrants (if using).
2. **Add Sweetener:** Add honey or maple syrup if you prefer a sweeter shake. Adjust according to your taste.
3. **Add Ice:** Add a handful of ice cubes for a thicker, colder shake.
4. **Blend:** Blend on high until smooth and creamy. If the shake is too thick, add more milk to achieve your desired consistency.
5. **Taste and Adjust:** Taste the shake and adjust the sweetness or blackcurrant flavor if needed by adding more honey or cordial.
6. **Serve:** Pour the shake into a glass. Optionally, garnish with fresh mint leaves or extra blackcurrants for a touch of elegance.

Enjoy your Blackcurrant Cordial Shake! It's a fruity and creamy treat that brings out the rich, tangy flavor of blackcurrants in a refreshing and indulgent shake.

Lemon Drizzle Cake Shake

Ingredients:

- 1 cup milk (dairy or non-dairy, such as almond or oat milk)
- 1/2 cup vanilla ice cream (or dairy-free ice cream)
- 1/2 cup Greek yogurt (plain or vanilla)
- 1/2 cup lemon cake (crumbled, store-bought or homemade)
- 2 tablespoons lemon curd (for extra lemon flavor)
- 1 tablespoon honey or maple syrup (adjust to taste)
- 1/4 teaspoon vanilla extract
- 1/4 teaspoon lemon zest (for added zing)
- Ice cubes (as needed)
- Optional: Whipped cream and additional lemon zest (for garnish)

Instructions:

1. **Prepare Lemon Cake:** If using store-bought lemon cake, crumble it into small pieces. If homemade, let it cool and crumble it.
2. **Blend Ingredients:** In a blender, combine the milk, vanilla ice cream, Greek yogurt, crumbled lemon cake, lemon curd, honey or maple syrup, vanilla extract, and lemon zest.
3. **Add Ice:** Add a handful of ice cubes for a thicker, colder shake.
4. **Blend:** Blend on high until smooth and creamy. If the shake is too thick, add more milk to reach your desired consistency.
5. **Taste and Adjust:** Taste the shake and adjust sweetness or lemon flavor if needed by adding more honey or lemon curd.
6. **Serve:** Pour the shake into a glass. Optionally, top with whipped cream and a sprinkle of additional lemon zest for a touch of extra flavor and elegance.

Enjoy your Lemon Drizzle Cake Shake! It's a creamy and tangy treat that combines the bright citrus flavor of lemon drizzle cake with the smooth, refreshing texture of a milkshake.

Gingerbread Biscuit Shake

Ingredients:

- 1 cup milk (dairy or non-dairy, such as almond or oat milk)
- 1/2 cup vanilla ice cream (or dairy-free ice cream)
- 1/2 cup Greek yogurt (plain or vanilla)
- 4-6 gingerbread biscuits (crumbled)
- 1 tablespoon molasses or honey (for extra depth of flavor)
- 1/4 teaspoon ground ginger
- 1/4 teaspoon ground cinnamon
- 1/4 teaspoon vanilla extract
- Ice cubes (as needed)
- Optional: Whipped cream and extra crumbled gingerbread biscuits (for garnish)

Instructions:

1. **Crush Biscuits:** Crush the gingerbread biscuits into small pieces. You can do this using a food processor or by placing them in a sealed bag and crushing them with a rolling pin.
2. **Blend Ingredients:** In a blender, combine the milk, vanilla ice cream, Greek yogurt, crumbled gingerbread biscuits, molasses or honey, ground ginger, ground cinnamon, and vanilla extract.
3. **Add Ice:** Add a handful of ice cubes to the blender for a thicker, colder shake.
4. **Blend:** Blend on high until smooth and creamy. If the shake is too thick, add more milk to reach your desired consistency.
5. **Taste and Adjust:** Taste the shake and adjust the sweetness or spice if needed by adding more molasses, honey, or spices.
6. **Serve:** Pour the shake into a glass. Optionally, top with whipped cream and a sprinkle of extra crumbled gingerbread biscuits for added texture and indulgence.

Enjoy your Gingerbread Biscuit Shake! It's a creamy, spiced treat that brings the comforting flavors of gingerbread biscuits into a refreshing milkshake.

Victoria Sponge Shake

Ingredients:

- 1 cup milk (dairy or non-dairy, such as almond or oat milk)
- 1/2 cup vanilla ice cream (or dairy-free ice cream)
- 1/2 cup Greek yogurt (plain or vanilla)
- 1/2 cup crumbled Victoria sponge cake (store-bought or homemade)
- 2 tablespoons strawberry jam or preserves (for a classic touch)
- 1 tablespoon powdered sugar (optional, for extra sweetness)
- 1/4 teaspoon vanilla extract
- Ice cubes (as needed)
- Optional: Whipped cream and extra strawberry jam (for garnish)

Instructions:

1. **Prepare Cake:** If using store-bought Victoria sponge cake, crumble it into small pieces. If homemade, let it cool before crumbling.
2. **Blend Ingredients:** In a blender, combine the milk, vanilla ice cream, Greek yogurt, crumbled Victoria sponge cake, strawberry jam, powdered sugar (if using), and vanilla extract.
3. **Add Ice:** Add a handful of ice cubes for a thicker, colder shake.
4. **Blend:** Blend on high until smooth and creamy. If the shake is too thick, add more milk to achieve your desired consistency.
5. **Taste and Adjust:** Taste the shake and adjust sweetness if needed by adding more powdered sugar or strawberry jam.
6. **Serve:** Pour the shake into a glass. Optionally, top with whipped cream and a dollop of extra strawberry jam for a classic touch.

Enjoy your Victoria Sponge Shake! It's a creamy and nostalgic treat that beautifully blends the flavors of the classic British cake with the refreshing texture of a milkshake.

Chocolate Digestive Shake

Ingredients:

- 1 cup milk (dairy or non-dairy, such as almond or oat milk)
- 1/2 cup vanilla ice cream (or dairy-free ice cream)
- 1/2 cup Greek yogurt (plain or vanilla)
- 4-6 chocolate digestives (crumbled)
- 2 tablespoons chocolate syrup (adjust to taste)
- 1 tablespoon honey or maple syrup (optional, for extra sweetness)
- 1/4 teaspoon vanilla extract
- Ice cubes (as needed)
- Optional: Whipped cream and extra crumbled chocolate digestives (for garnish)

Instructions:

1. **Crush Digestives:** Crush the chocolate digestives into small pieces. You can do this using a food processor or by placing them in a sealed bag and crushing them with a rolling pin.
2. **Blend Ingredients:** In a blender, combine the milk, vanilla ice cream, Greek yogurt, crumbled chocolate digestives, chocolate syrup, honey or maple syrup (if using), and vanilla extract.
3. **Add Ice:** Add a handful of ice cubes for a thicker, colder shake.
4. **Blend:** Blend on high until smooth and creamy. If the shake is too thick, add more milk to reach your desired consistency.
5. **Taste and Adjust:** Taste the shake and adjust sweetness or chocolate flavor if needed by adding more honey or chocolate syrup.
6. **Serve:** Pour the shake into a glass. Optionally, top with whipped cream and a sprinkle of extra crumbled chocolate digestives for added texture and indulgence.

Enjoy your Chocolate Digestive Shake! It's a decadent treat that combines the creamy texture of a milkshake with the rich, chocolatey goodness of chocolate digestives, making for a truly delightful dessert.

Classic British Scone Shake

Ingredients:

- 1 cup milk (dairy or non-dairy, such as almond or oat milk)
- 1/2 cup vanilla ice cream (or dairy-free ice cream)
- 1/2 cup Greek yogurt (plain or vanilla)
- 1 cup crumbled scone (plain or fruit scone; store-bought or homemade)
- 2 tablespoons clotted cream or heavy cream (for richness)
- 2 tablespoons strawberry jam or preserves (for a classic scone topping)
- 1 tablespoon honey or maple syrup (optional, for extra sweetness)
- 1/4 teaspoon vanilla extract
- Ice cubes (as needed)
- Optional: Whipped cream and extra strawberry jam or fresh berries (for garnish)

Instructions:

1. **Prepare Scone:** If using store-bought scones, crumble them into small pieces. If homemade, let them cool before crumbling.
2. **Blend Ingredients:** In a blender, combine the milk, vanilla ice cream, Greek yogurt, crumbled scone, clotted cream or heavy cream, strawberry jam, honey or maple syrup (if using), and vanilla extract.
3. **Add Ice:** Add a handful of ice cubes for a thicker, colder shake.
4. **Blend:** Blend on high until smooth and creamy. If the shake is too thick, add more milk to achieve your desired consistency.
5. **Taste and Adjust:** Taste the shake and adjust sweetness or jam flavor if needed by adding more honey or strawberry jam.
6. **Serve:** Pour the shake into a glass. Optionally, top with whipped cream and a dollop of extra strawberry jam or fresh berries for added flavor and a touch of elegance.

Enjoy your Classic British Scone Shake! It's a creamy, nostalgic treat that beautifully blends the flavors of traditional British scones with the refreshing texture of a milkshake.

Minced Pie Shake

Ingredients:

- 1 cup milk (dairy or non-dairy, such as almond or oat milk)
- 1/2 cup vanilla ice cream (or dairy-free ice cream)
- 1/2 cup Greek yogurt (plain or vanilla)
- 1 cup crumbled mince pies (store-bought or homemade)
- 2 tablespoons mincemeat (for extra mincemeat flavor)
- 1 tablespoon honey or maple syrup (optional, for extra sweetness)
- 1/4 teaspoon ground cinnamon
- 1/4 teaspoon ground nutmeg
- 1/4 teaspoon vanilla extract
- Ice cubes (as needed)
- Optional: Whipped cream, extra crumbled mince pie, or a sprinkle of cinnamon (for garnish)

Instructions:

1. **Prepare Mince Pies:** If using store-bought mince pies, crumble them into small pieces. If homemade, let them cool before crumbling.
2. **Blend Ingredients:** In a blender, combine the milk, vanilla ice cream, Greek yogurt, crumbled mince pies, mincemeat, honey or maple syrup (if using), ground cinnamon, ground nutmeg, and vanilla extract.
3. **Add Ice:** Add a handful of ice cubes for a thicker, colder shake.
4. **Blend:** Blend on high until smooth and creamy. If the shake is too thick, add more milk to achieve your desired consistency.
5. **Taste and Adjust:** Taste the shake and adjust sweetness or spice if needed by adding more honey or spices.
6. **Serve:** Pour the shake into a glass. Optionally, top with whipped cream and a sprinkle of extra crumbled mince pie or a dash of cinnamon for added festivity and flavor.

Enjoy your Minced Pie Shake! It's a creamy, spiced treat that captures the essence of mince pies in a refreshing and indulgent milkshake.

Bread and Butter Pudding Shake

Ingredients:

- 1 cup milk (dairy or non-dairy, such as almond or oat milk)
- 1/2 cup vanilla ice cream (or dairy-free ice cream)
- 1/2 cup Greek yogurt (plain or vanilla)
- 1 cup crumbled bread and butter pudding (store-bought or homemade, cooled)
- 1 tablespoon raisins or sultanas (optional, for added texture and flavor)
- 1 tablespoon honey or maple syrup (optional, for extra sweetness)
- 1/4 teaspoon ground cinnamon
- 1/4 teaspoon ground nutmeg
- 1/4 teaspoon vanilla extract
- Ice cubes (as needed)
- Optional: Whipped cream and a sprinkle of ground cinnamon or extra raisins (for garnish)

Instructions:

1. **Prepare Pudding:** If using store-bought bread and butter pudding, crumble it into small pieces. If homemade, let it cool before crumbling.
2. **Blend Ingredients:** In a blender, combine the milk, vanilla ice cream, Greek yogurt, crumbled bread and butter pudding, raisins or sultanas (if using), honey or maple syrup (if using), ground cinnamon, ground nutmeg, and vanilla extract.
3. **Add Ice:** Add a handful of ice cubes for a thicker, colder shake.
4. **Blend:** Blend on high until smooth and creamy. If the shake is too thick, add more milk to achieve your desired consistency.
5. **Taste and Adjust:** Taste the shake and adjust sweetness or spice if needed by adding more honey or spices.
6. **Serve:** Pour the shake into a glass. Optionally, top with whipped cream and a sprinkle of ground cinnamon or extra raisins for added flavor and texture.

Enjoy your Bread and Butter Pudding Shake! It's a creamy, nostalgic treat that brings the comforting flavors of a classic British dessert into a refreshing and indulgent milkshake.

Pimm's Summer Shake

Ingredients:

- 1 cup milk (dairy or non-dairy, such as almond or oat milk)
- 1/2 cup vanilla ice cream (or dairy-free ice cream)
- 1/2 cup Greek yogurt (plain or vanilla)
- 1/4 cup Pimm's No. 1 (adjust to taste, and ensure you're using responsibly)
- 1/4 cup mixed fresh fruit (such as strawberries, cucumber, orange slices, and mint leaves)
- 1 tablespoon honey or maple syrup (optional, for extra sweetness)
- 1/4 teaspoon vanilla extract
- Ice cubes (as needed)
- Optional: Fresh mint leaves and extra fruit slices (for garnish)

Instructions:

1. **Prepare Fruit:** Wash and chop the mixed fresh fruit into small pieces. If using cucumber, slice thinly.
2. **Blend Ingredients:** In a blender, combine the milk, vanilla ice cream, Greek yogurt, Pimm's No. 1, chopped fruit, honey or maple syrup (if using), and vanilla extract.
3. **Add Ice:** Add a handful of ice cubes for a thicker, colder shake.
4. **Blend:** Blend on high until smooth and creamy. If the shake is too thick, add more milk to achieve your desired consistency.
5. **Taste and Adjust:** Taste the shake and adjust sweetness or fruit flavor if needed by adding more honey or adjusting the fruit proportions.
6. **Serve:** Pour the shake into a glass. Optionally, garnish with fresh mint leaves and additional fruit slices for a decorative and flavorful touch.

Enjoy your Pimm's Summer Shake! It's a delightful and refreshing treat that combines the classic flavors of Pimm's with the creamy texture of a milkshake, perfect for summer or any time you want a taste of something special.

Cherry Bakewell Shake

Ingredients:

- 1 cup milk (dairy or non-dairy, such as almond or oat milk)
- 1/2 cup vanilla ice cream (or dairy-free ice cream)
- 1/2 cup Greek yogurt (plain or vanilla)
- 1/2 cup crumbled Bakewell tart (store-bought or homemade, cooled)
- 2 tablespoons cherry jam or preserves
- 1 tablespoon almond extract or almond butter
- 1 tablespoon honey or maple syrup (optional, for extra sweetness)
- 1/4 teaspoon ground almond (optional, for extra almond flavor)
- Ice cubes (as needed)
- Optional: Whipped cream and extra cherry jam or sliced almonds (for garnish)

Instructions:

1. **Prepare Tart:** If using a store-bought Bakewell tart, crumble it into small pieces. If homemade, let it cool before crumbling.
2. **Blend Ingredients:** In a blender, combine the milk, vanilla ice cream, Greek yogurt, crumbled Bakewell tart, cherry jam, almond extract or almond butter, honey or maple syrup (if using), and ground almond (if using).
3. **Add Ice:** Add a handful of ice cubes for a thicker, colder shake.
4. **Blend:** Blend on high until smooth and creamy. If the shake is too thick, add more milk to achieve your desired consistency.
5. **Taste and Adjust:** Taste the shake and adjust sweetness or flavor if needed by adding more honey, cherry jam, or almond extract.
6. **Serve:** Pour the shake into a glass. Optionally, top with whipped cream and a drizzle of extra cherry jam or a sprinkle of sliced almonds for added texture and indulgence.

Enjoy your Cherry Bakewell Shake! It's a creamy, nostalgic treat that captures the delicious flavors of a Cherry Bakewell tart in a refreshing milkshake.

Jelly and Ice Cream Shake

Ingredients:

- 1 cup milk (dairy or non-dairy, such as almond or oat milk)
- 1/2 cup vanilla ice cream (or dairy-free ice cream)
- 1/2 cup Greek yogurt (plain or vanilla)
- 1/2 cup jelly (flavor of your choice; strawberry, raspberry, or any other preferred flavor)
- 1 tablespoon honey or maple syrup (optional, for extra sweetness)
- 1/4 teaspoon vanilla extract
- Ice cubes (as needed)
- Optional: Whipped cream and extra jelly cubes or sprinkles (for garnish)

Instructions:

1. **Prepare Jelly:** If using homemade jelly, ensure it is set and cut into small pieces. If using store-bought jelly, make sure it's firm. For best results, slightly soften the jelly in the microwave or let it come to room temperature for easier blending.
2. **Blend Ingredients:** In a blender, combine the milk, vanilla ice cream, Greek yogurt, jelly, honey or maple syrup (if using), and vanilla extract.
3. **Add Ice:** Add a handful of ice cubes for a thicker, colder shake.
4. **Blend:** Blend on high until smooth and creamy. If the shake is too thick, add more milk to achieve your desired consistency.
5. **Taste and Adjust:** Taste the shake and adjust sweetness if needed by adding more honey or maple syrup.
6. **Serve:** Pour the shake into a glass. Optionally, top with whipped cream and garnish with extra jelly cubes or sprinkles for a fun and colorful touch.

Enjoy your Jelly and Ice Cream Shake! It's a delightful treat that combines the playful flavors of jelly with the creamy richness of ice cream in a fun and refreshing milkshake.

Toad in the Hole Shake

Ingredients:

- 1 cup milk (dairy or non-dairy, such as almond or oat milk)
- 1/2 cup vanilla ice cream (or dairy-free ice cream)
- 1/2 cup Greek yogurt (plain or vanilla)
- 1/2 cup crumbled Yorkshire pudding (store-bought or homemade, cooled)
- 2 tablespoons toad-in-the-hole sausage or sausage-flavored syrup (optional, for an authentic touch)
- 1 tablespoon honey or maple syrup (optional, for extra sweetness)
- 1/4 teaspoon ground cinnamon
- 1/4 teaspoon vanilla extract
- Ice cubes (as needed)
- Optional: Whipped cream and extra crumbled Yorkshire pudding (for garnish)

Instructions:

1. **Prepare Yorkshire Pudding:** If using store-bought Yorkshire pudding, crumble it into small pieces. If homemade, let it cool and then crumble.
2. **Blend Ingredients:** In a blender, combine the milk, vanilla ice cream, Greek yogurt, crumbled Yorkshire pudding, sausage-flavored syrup (if using), honey or maple syrup (if using), ground cinnamon, and vanilla extract.
3. **Add Ice:** Add a handful of ice cubes for a thicker, colder shake.
4. **Blend:** Blend on high until smooth and creamy. If the shake is too thick, add more milk to achieve your desired consistency.
5. **Taste and Adjust:** Taste the shake and adjust sweetness or spice if needed by adding more honey or cinnamon.
6. **Serve:** Pour the shake into a glass. Optionally, top with whipped cream and a sprinkle of extra crumbled Yorkshire pudding for added texture and a playful touch.

Enjoy your Toad in the Hole Shake! It's a fun, creamy treat that brings the savory flavors of the classic British dish into a refreshing and indulgent milkshake.

Plum Pudding Shake

Ingredients:

- 1 cup milk (dairy or non-dairy, such as almond or oat milk)
- 1/2 cup vanilla ice cream (or dairy-free ice cream)
- 1/2 cup Greek yogurt (plain or vanilla)
- 1 cup crumbled plum pudding (store-bought or homemade, cooled)
- 2 tablespoons fruit preserves (such as plum or apricot)
- 1 tablespoon honey or maple syrup (optional, for extra sweetness)
- 1/4 teaspoon ground cinnamon
- 1/4 teaspoon ground nutmeg
- 1/4 teaspoon vanilla extract
- Ice cubes (as needed)
- Optional: Whipped cream and extra crumbled plum pudding or a sprinkle of ground spices (for garnish)

Instructions:

1. **Prepare Plum Pudding:** If using store-bought plum pudding, crumble it into small pieces. If homemade, ensure it is cool and crumbled before adding.
2. **Blend Ingredients:** In a blender, combine the milk, vanilla ice cream, Greek yogurt, crumbled plum pudding, fruit preserves, honey or maple syrup (if using), ground cinnamon, ground nutmeg, and vanilla extract.
3. **Add Ice:** Add a handful of ice cubes for a thicker, colder shake.
4. **Blend:** Blend on high until smooth and creamy. If the shake is too thick, add more milk to achieve your desired consistency.
5. **Taste and Adjust:** Taste the shake and adjust sweetness or spice as needed by adding more honey or spices.
6. **Serve:** Pour the shake into a glass. Optionally, top with whipped cream and a sprinkle of extra crumbled plum pudding or a dash of ground cinnamon and nutmeg for added flavor and festive flair.

Enjoy your Plum Pudding Shake! It's a creamy, indulgent treat that brings the rich, fruity flavors of a traditional plum pudding into a refreshing milkshake.

English Breakfast Tea Shake

Ingredients:

- 1 cup milk (dairy or non-dairy, such as almond or oat milk)
- 1/2 cup vanilla ice cream (or dairy-free ice cream)
- 1/2 cup Greek yogurt (plain or vanilla)
- 1-2 teaspoons loose English Breakfast tea leaves or 1-2 tea bags (for steeping)
- 1 tablespoon honey or maple syrup (optional, for extra sweetness)
- 1/4 teaspoon vanilla extract
- Ice cubes (as needed)
- Optional: Whipped cream and a dusting of ground cinnamon or tea leaves (for garnish)

Instructions:

1. **Brew Tea:** Brew the English Breakfast tea by steeping the tea leaves or tea bags in a small amount of hot water (about 1/4 cup) for 3-5 minutes. Remove the tea leaves or bags and let the tea cool to room temperature.
2. **Blend Ingredients:** In a blender, combine the milk, vanilla ice cream, Greek yogurt, cooled tea, honey or maple syrup (if using), and vanilla extract.
3. **Add Ice:** Add a handful of ice cubes for a thicker, colder shake.
4. **Blend:** Blend on high until smooth and creamy. If the shake is too thick, add more milk to achieve your desired consistency.
5. **Taste and Adjust:** Taste the shake and adjust sweetness if needed by adding more honey or maple syrup.
6. **Serve:** Pour the shake into a glass. Optionally, top with whipped cream and a dusting of ground cinnamon or extra tea leaves for a decorative touch.

Enjoy your English Breakfast Tea Shake! It's a sophisticated and creamy treat that beautifully blends the bold flavors of English Breakfast tea with the rich, indulgent texture of a milkshake.

Fruit and Nut Bar Shake

Ingredients:

- 1 cup milk (dairy or non-dairy, such as almond or oat milk)
- 1/2 cup vanilla ice cream (or dairy-free ice cream)
- 1/2 cup Greek yogurt (plain or vanilla)
- 1 cup crumbled fruit and nut bar (such as a granola bar with nuts and dried fruit; store-bought or homemade)
- 2 tablespoons mixed dried fruit (such as raisins, apricots, or cranberries)
- 2 tablespoons chopped nuts (such as almonds, walnuts, or cashews)
- 1 tablespoon honey or maple syrup (optional, for extra sweetness)
- 1/4 teaspoon vanilla extract
- Ice cubes (as needed)
- Optional: Whipped cream and extra crumbled fruit and nut bar or a sprinkle of chopped nuts (for garnish)

Instructions:

1. **Prepare Fruit and Nut Bar:** If using store-bought fruit and nut bars, crumble them into small pieces. If homemade, let them cool and crumble.
2. **Blend Ingredients:** In a blender, combine the milk, vanilla ice cream, Greek yogurt, crumbled fruit and nut bar, dried fruit, chopped nuts, honey or maple syrup (if using), and vanilla extract.
3. **Add Ice:** Add a handful of ice cubes for a thicker, colder shake.
4. **Blend:** Blend on high until smooth and creamy. If the shake is too thick, add more milk to reach your desired consistency.
5. **Taste and Adjust:** Taste the shake and adjust sweetness or flavor if needed by adding more honey or nuts.
6. **Serve:** Pour the shake into a glass. Optionally, top with whipped cream and a sprinkle of extra crumbled fruit and nut bar or chopped nuts for added texture and visual appeal.

Enjoy your Fruit and Nut Bar Shake! It's a creamy, satisfying treat that combines the wholesome flavors of fruit and nut bars with the rich, indulgent texture of a milkshake.

Bakewell Tart Shake

Ingredients:

- 1 cup milk (dairy or non-dairy, such as almond or oat milk)
- 1/2 cup vanilla ice cream (or dairy-free ice cream)
- 1/2 cup Greek yogurt (plain or vanilla)
- 1 cup crumbled Bakewell tart (store-bought or homemade, cooled)
- 2 tablespoons cherry jam or preserves
- 1 tablespoon almond extract or almond butter
- 1 tablespoon honey or maple syrup (optional, for extra sweetness)
- 1/4 teaspoon ground almond (optional, for extra almond flavor)
- Ice cubes (as needed)
- Optional: Whipped cream and extra cherry jam or sliced almonds (for garnish)

Instructions:

1. **Prepare Bakewell Tart:** If using store-bought Bakewell tart, crumble it into small pieces. If homemade, ensure it is cooled and crumbled before adding to the blender.
2. **Blend Ingredients:** In a blender, combine the milk, vanilla ice cream, Greek yogurt, crumbled Bakewell tart, cherry jam, almond extract or almond butter, honey or maple syrup (if using), and ground almond (if using).
3. **Add Ice:** Add a handful of ice cubes for a thicker, colder shake.
4. **Blend:** Blend on high until smooth and creamy. If the shake is too thick, add more milk to achieve your desired consistency.
5. **Taste and Adjust:** Taste the shake and adjust sweetness or flavor as needed by adding more honey, cherry jam, or almond extract.
6. **Serve:** Pour the shake into a glass. Optionally, top with whipped cream and a drizzle of extra cherry jam or a sprinkle of sliced almonds for added texture and a decorative touch.

Enjoy your Bakewell Tart Shake! It's a creamy, indulgent treat that captures the delicious flavors of a traditional Bakewell tart in a refreshing and satisfying milkshake.

Mince Pie Shake

Ingredients:

- 1 cup milk (dairy or non-dairy, such as almond or oat milk)
- 1/2 cup vanilla ice cream (or dairy-free ice cream)
- 1/2 cup Greek yogurt (plain or vanilla)
- 1 cup crumbled mince pie (store-bought or homemade, cooled)
- 2 tablespoons mincemeat (for extra mincemeat flavor)
- 1 tablespoon honey or maple syrup (optional, for extra sweetness)
- 1/4 teaspoon ground cinnamon
- 1/4 teaspoon ground nutmeg
- 1/4 teaspoon ground cloves (optional)
- 1/4 teaspoon vanilla extract
- Ice cubes (as needed)
- Optional: Whipped cream and extra crumbled mince pie or a sprinkle of ground spices (for garnish)

Instructions:

1. **Prepare Mince Pie:** If using store-bought mince pie, crumble it into small pieces. If homemade, ensure it's cooled and crumbled before adding to the blender.
2. **Blend Ingredients:** In a blender, combine the milk, vanilla ice cream, Greek yogurt, crumbled mince pie, mincemeat, honey or maple syrup (if using), ground cinnamon, ground nutmeg, ground cloves (if using), and vanilla extract.
3. **Add Ice:** Add a handful of ice cubes for a thicker, colder shake.
4. **Blend:** Blend on high until smooth and creamy. If the shake is too thick, add more milk to achieve your desired consistency.
5. **Taste and Adjust:** Taste the shake and adjust sweetness or spices as needed by adding more honey or spices.
6. **Serve:** Pour the shake into a glass. Optionally, top with whipped cream and a sprinkle of extra crumbled mince pie or a dash of ground spices for added flavor and a festive touch.

Enjoy your Mince Pie Shake! It's a rich and creamy treat that brings the comforting flavors of traditional mince pies into a refreshing and indulgent milkshake.

Scone and Clotted Cream Shake

Ingredients:

- 1 cup milk (dairy or non-dairy, such as almond or oat milk)
- 1/2 cup vanilla ice cream (or dairy-free ice cream)
- 1/2 cup Greek yogurt (plain or vanilla)
- 1 cup crumbled scone (store-bought or homemade, cooled; plain or fruit-flavored scones work well)
- 2 tablespoons clotted cream
- 1 tablespoon honey or maple syrup (optional, for extra sweetness)
- 1/4 teaspoon vanilla extract
- Ice cubes (as needed)
- Optional: Whipped cream and extra crumbled scone or a dollop of clotted cream (for garnish)

Instructions:

1. **Prepare Scone:** If using a store-bought scone, crumble it into small pieces. If homemade, ensure it is cooled and crumbled before adding to the blender.
2. **Blend Ingredients:** In a blender, combine the milk, vanilla ice cream, Greek yogurt, crumbled scone, clotted cream, honey or maple syrup (if using), and vanilla extract.
3. **Add Ice:** Add a handful of ice cubes for a thicker, colder shake.
4. **Blend:** Blend on high until smooth and creamy. If the shake is too thick, add more milk to achieve your desired consistency.
5. **Taste and Adjust:** Taste the shake and adjust sweetness if needed by adding more honey or syrup.
6. **Serve:** Pour the shake into a glass. Optionally, top with whipped cream and a sprinkle of extra crumbled scone or a dollop of clotted cream for added texture and indulgence.

Enjoy your Scone and Clotted Cream Shake! It's a luxurious and creamy treat that brings the classic flavors of a scone with clotted cream into a refreshing and indulgent milkshake.

Welsh Cakes Shake

Ingredients:

- 1 cup milk (dairy or non-dairy, such as almond or oat milk)
- 1/2 cup vanilla ice cream (or dairy-free ice cream)
- 1/2 cup Greek yogurt (plain or vanilla)
- 1 cup crumbled Welsh cakes (store-bought or homemade, cooled)
- 1/4 cup raisins or currants
- 1 tablespoon honey or maple syrup (optional, for extra sweetness)
- 1/4 teaspoon ground cinnamon
- 1/4 teaspoon ground nutmeg
- 1/4 teaspoon vanilla extract
- Ice cubes (as needed)
- Optional: Whipped cream and extra crumbled Welsh cakes or a sprinkle of cinnamon sugar (for garnish)

Instructions:

1. **Prepare Welsh Cakes:** If using store-bought Welsh cakes, crumble them into small pieces. If homemade, ensure they are cooled and crumbled before adding to the blender.
2. **Blend Ingredients:** In a blender, combine the milk, vanilla ice cream, Greek yogurt, crumbled Welsh cakes, raisins or currants, honey or maple syrup (if using), ground cinnamon, ground nutmeg, and vanilla extract.
3. **Add Ice:** Add a handful of ice cubes for a thicker, colder shake.
4. **Blend:** Blend on high until smooth and creamy. If the shake is too thick, add more milk to achieve your desired consistency.
5. **Taste and Adjust:** Taste the shake and adjust sweetness or spice as needed by adding more honey or spices.
6. **Serve:** Pour the shake into a glass. Optionally, top with whipped cream and a sprinkle of extra crumbled Welsh cakes or a dash of cinnamon sugar for added texture and a touch of indulgence.

Enjoy your Welsh Cakes Shake! It's a creamy, nostalgic treat that brings the delightful flavors of Welsh cakes into a refreshing and satisfying milkshake.

Rhubarb Fool Shake

Ingredients:

- 1 cup milk (dairy or non-dairy, such as almond or oat milk)
- 1/2 cup vanilla ice cream (or dairy-free ice cream)
- 1/2 cup Greek yogurt (plain or vanilla)
- 1 cup rhubarb compote (store-bought or homemade)
- 2 tablespoons honey or maple syrup (optional, for extra sweetness)
- 1/4 teaspoon vanilla extract
- Ice cubes (as needed)
- Optional: Whipped cream and extra rhubarb compote or fresh rhubarb slices (for garnish)

Instructions:

1. **Prepare Rhubarb Compote:** If making homemade rhubarb compote, cook chopped rhubarb with a bit of sugar until tender and thickened. Let it cool before using. Alternatively, use store-bought rhubarb compote.
2. **Blend Ingredients:** In a blender, combine the milk, vanilla ice cream, Greek yogurt, rhubarb compote, honey or maple syrup (if using), and vanilla extract.
3. **Add Ice:** Add a handful of ice cubes for a thicker, colder shake.
4. **Blend:** Blend on high until smooth and creamy. If the shake is too thick, add more milk to achieve your desired consistency.
5. **Taste and Adjust:** Taste the shake and adjust sweetness if needed by adding more honey or syrup.
6. **Serve:** Pour the shake into a glass. Optionally, top with whipped cream and a dollop of extra rhubarb compote or fresh rhubarb slices for added flavor and a decorative touch.

Enjoy your Rhubarb Fool Shake! It's a creamy, tangy treat that captures the essence of the classic rhubarb fool dessert in a refreshing and indulgent milkshake.

Chocolate and Orange Jaffa Cake Shake

Ingredients:

- 1 cup milk (dairy or non-dairy, such as almond or oat milk)
- 1/2 cup vanilla ice cream (or dairy-free ice cream)
- 1/2 cup Greek yogurt (plain or vanilla)
- 6-8 Jaffa Cakes (or similar chocolate-covered orange-flavored biscuits)
- 2 tablespoons orange marmalade (for an extra burst of orange flavor)
- 1 tablespoon honey or maple syrup (optional, for extra sweetness)
- 1/4 teaspoon vanilla extract
- Ice cubes (as needed)
- Optional: Whipped cream and extra crushed Jaffa Cakes or a drizzle of chocolate syrup (for garnish)

Instructions:

1. **Prepare Jaffa Cakes:** If using store-bought Jaffa Cakes, crumble them into small pieces. You can do this using a food processor or by placing them in a sealed bag and crushing them with a rolling pin.
2. **Blend Ingredients:** In a blender, combine the milk, vanilla ice cream, Greek yogurt, crumbled Jaffa Cakes, orange marmalade, honey or maple syrup (if using), and vanilla extract.
3. **Add Ice:** Add a handful of ice cubes for a thicker, colder shake.
4. **Blend:** Blend on high until smooth and creamy. If the shake is too thick, add more milk to reach your desired consistency.
5. **Taste and Adjust:** Taste the shake and adjust sweetness or orange flavor if needed by adding more honey or marmalade.
6. **Serve:** Pour the shake into a glass. Optionally, top with whipped cream and a sprinkle of extra crushed Jaffa Cakes or a drizzle of chocolate syrup for added flavor and a decorative touch.

Enjoy your Chocolate and Orange Jaffa Cake Shake! It's a creamy, indulgent treat that combines the rich flavors of chocolate and orange with the classic crunch of Jaffa Cakes in a refreshing milkshake.

Summer Fruits Eton Mess Shake

Ingredients:

- 1 cup milk (dairy or non-dairy, such as almond or oat milk)
- 1/2 cup vanilla ice cream (or dairy-free ice cream)
- 1/2 cup Greek yogurt (plain or vanilla)
- 1 cup mixed summer fruits (such as strawberries, raspberries, blueberries, and blackberries; fresh or frozen)
- 3-4 meringue nests (crushed)
- 2 tablespoons honey or maple syrup (optional, for extra sweetness)
- 1/4 teaspoon vanilla extract
- Ice cubes (as needed)
- Optional: Whipped cream and extra fruit or crushed meringues (for garnish)

Instructions:

1. **Prepare Fruits:** If using fresh fruits, wash and hull them as needed. If using frozen fruits, let them thaw slightly before use.
2. **Blend Ingredients:** In a blender, combine the milk, vanilla ice cream, Greek yogurt, mixed summer fruits, crushed meringue nests, honey or maple syrup (if using), and vanilla extract.
3. **Add Ice:** Add a handful of ice cubes for a thicker, colder shake.
4. **Blend:** Blend on high until smooth and creamy. If the shake is too thick, add more milk to achieve your desired consistency.
5. **Taste and Adjust:** Taste the shake and adjust sweetness if needed by adding more honey or syrup.
6. **Serve:** Pour the shake into a glass. Optionally, top with whipped cream and a sprinkle of extra crushed meringues or fresh summer fruits for added texture and a decorative touch.

Enjoy your Summer Fruits Eton Mess Shake! It's a creamy, fruity treat that captures the essence of the classic Eton Mess dessert in a refreshing milkshake.

Spicy Apple and Cinnamon Shake

Ingredients:

- 1 cup milk (dairy or non-dairy, such as almond or oat milk)
- 1/2 cup vanilla ice cream (or dairy-free ice cream)
- 1/2 cup Greek yogurt (plain or vanilla)
- 1 medium apple (peeled, cored, and chopped; for a spicier kick, use a tart apple like Granny Smith)
- 1/4 teaspoon ground cinnamon
- 1/4 teaspoon ground nutmeg
- 1/4 teaspoon ground ginger (optional, for extra spice)
- 1 tablespoon honey or maple syrup (optional, for extra sweetness)
- Ice cubes (as needed)
- Optional: Whipped cream and a sprinkle of cinnamon sugar (for garnish)

Instructions:

1. **Prepare Apple:** Peel, core, and chop the apple into small pieces. For a smoother texture, you can also lightly cook the apple pieces until soft and let them cool.
2. **Blend Ingredients:** In a blender, combine the milk, vanilla ice cream, Greek yogurt, chopped apple, ground cinnamon, ground nutmeg, ground ginger (if using), and honey or maple syrup (if using).
3. **Add Ice:** Add a handful of ice cubes for a thicker, colder shake.
4. **Blend:** Blend on high until smooth and creamy. If the shake is too thick, add more milk to achieve your desired consistency.
5. **Taste and Adjust:** Taste the shake and adjust sweetness or spice as needed by adding more honey, syrup, or spices.
6. **Serve:** Pour the shake into a glass. Optionally, top with whipped cream and a sprinkle of cinnamon sugar for added flavor and a decorative touch.

Enjoy your Spicy Apple and Cinnamon Shake! It's a creamy, spiced treat that brings the cozy flavors of apple pie into a refreshing and satisfying milkshake.

Raspberry Ripple Shake

Ingredients:

- 1 cup milk (dairy or non-dairy, such as almond or oat milk)
- 1/2 cup vanilla ice cream (or dairy-free ice cream)
- 1/2 cup Greek yogurt (plain or vanilla)
- 1 cup fresh or frozen raspberries
- 2 tablespoons honey or maple syrup (optional, for extra sweetness)
- 1/4 teaspoon vanilla extract
- Ice cubes (as needed)
- Optional: Whipped cream and extra raspberries (for garnish)

Instructions:

1. **Prepare Raspberry Sauce:** In a small saucepan, heat the raspberries over medium heat until they start to break down and release their juices, about 5 minutes. You can add a tablespoon of honey or maple syrup if you like it sweeter. Once softened, let it cool slightly, then blend until smooth. Alternatively, you can use store-bought raspberry sauce or jam.
2. **Blend Shake Base:** In a blender, combine the milk, vanilla ice cream, Greek yogurt, and vanilla extract.
3. **Add Ice:** Add a handful of ice cubes for a thicker, colder shake.
4. **Blend:** Blend on high until smooth and creamy. If the shake is too thick, add more milk to reach your desired consistency.
5. **Ripple Effect:** Pour the shake into a glass, then gently swirl in some of the raspberry sauce using a spoon or straw to create a ripple effect. You can also layer the shake with the raspberry sauce if you prefer a more dramatic swirl.
6. **Serve:** Optionally, top with whipped cream and extra raspberries for a decorative touch.

Enjoy your Raspberry Ripple Shake! It's a refreshing, creamy treat with the perfect blend of smooth vanilla and tart raspberry flavors.

Chocolate Mint Aero Shake

Ingredients:

- 1 cup milk (dairy or non-dairy, such as almond or oat milk)
- 1/2 cup vanilla ice cream (or dairy-free ice cream)
- 1/2 cup Greek yogurt (plain or vanilla)
- 3-4 Aero mint chocolate bars (chopped; or use a similar mint chocolate bar)
- 2 tablespoons chocolate syrup
- 1/4 teaspoon mint extract (adjust to taste; you can also use mint chocolate syrup for a stronger mint flavor)
- Ice cubes (as needed)
- Optional: Whipped cream and extra chopped Aero bars or a drizzle of chocolate syrup (for garnish)

Instructions:

1. **Prepare Chocolate Bars:** Chop the Aero mint chocolate bars into small pieces. If you prefer a smoother shake, you can also blend the chocolate bars briefly before adding them to the shake.
2. **Blend Ingredients:** In a blender, combine the milk, vanilla ice cream, Greek yogurt, chopped Aero bars, chocolate syrup, and mint extract.
3. **Add Ice:** Add a handful of ice cubes for a thicker, colder shake.
4. **Blend:** Blend on high until smooth and creamy. If the shake is too thick, add more milk to reach your desired consistency.
5. **Taste and Adjust:** Taste the shake and adjust sweetness or mint flavor if needed by adding more chocolate syrup or mint extract.
6. **Serve:** Pour the shake into a glass. Optionally, top with whipped cream and a sprinkle of extra chopped Aero bars or a drizzle of chocolate syrup for a decorative touch.

Enjoy your Chocolate Mint Aero Shake! It's a creamy, indulgent treat that combines the refreshing flavors of mint chocolate with the rich texture of a milkshake.

Lemon Curd Shake

Ingredients:

- 1 cup milk (dairy or non-dairy, such as almond or oat milk)
- 1/2 cup vanilla ice cream (or dairy-free ice cream)
- 1/2 cup Greek yogurt (plain or vanilla)
- 1/4 cup lemon curd (store-bought or homemade)
- 1 tablespoon honey or maple syrup (optional, for extra sweetness)
- 1/4 teaspoon vanilla extract (optional)
- Ice cubes (as needed)
- Optional: Whipped cream and lemon zest or a small dollop of lemon curd (for garnish)

Instructions:

1. **Blend Ingredients:** In a blender, combine the milk, vanilla ice cream, Greek yogurt, and lemon curd.
2. **Add Sweetener and Flavor:** Add honey or maple syrup if you want extra sweetness, and vanilla extract if using.
3. **Add Ice:** Add a handful of ice cubes for a thicker, colder shake.
4. **Blend:** Blend on high until smooth and creamy. If the shake is too thick, add more milk to achieve your desired consistency.
5. **Taste and Adjust:** Taste the shake and adjust sweetness or lemon flavor if needed by adding more honey or lemon curd.
6. **Serve:** Pour the shake into a glass. Optionally, top with whipped cream and a sprinkle of lemon zest or a small dollop of lemon curd for a decorative touch.

Enjoy your Lemon Curd Shake! It's a creamy and tangy treat that captures the bright, citrusy flavors of lemon curd in a refreshing milkshake.

Caramel Shortbread Shake

Ingredients:

- 1 cup milk (dairy or non-dairy, such as almond or oat milk)
- 1/2 cup vanilla ice cream (or dairy-free ice cream)
- 1/2 cup Greek yogurt (plain or vanilla)
- 6-8 shortbread cookies (crumbled)
- 1/4 cup caramel sauce (store-bought or homemade)
- 1 tablespoon honey or maple syrup (optional, for extra sweetness)
- 1/4 teaspoon vanilla extract
- Ice cubes (as needed)
- Optional: Whipped cream, extra caramel sauce, and additional crumbled shortbread cookies (for garnish)

Instructions:

1. **Prepare Shortbread:** If using store-bought shortbread cookies, crumble them into small pieces. You can do this using a food processor or by placing them in a sealed bag and crushing them with a rolling pin.
2. **Blend Ingredients:** In a blender, combine the milk, vanilla ice cream, Greek yogurt, crumbled shortbread cookies, caramel sauce, honey or maple syrup (if using), and vanilla extract.
3. **Add Ice:** Add a handful of ice cubes for a thicker, colder shake.
4. **Blend:** Blend on high until smooth and creamy. If the shake is too thick, add more milk to reach your desired consistency.
5. **Taste and Adjust:** Taste the shake and adjust sweetness if needed by adding more caramel sauce or honey.
6. **Serve:** Pour the shake into a glass. Optionally, top with whipped cream, a drizzle of extra caramel sauce, and a sprinkle of additional crumbled shortbread cookies for added texture and a decorative touch.

Enjoy your Caramel Shortbread Shake! It's a rich, creamy treat that combines the delightful flavors of caramel and shortbread into a refreshing and satisfying milkshake.

Fruity Jam Roly-Poly Shake

Ingredients:

- 1 cup milk (dairy or non-dairy, such as almond or oat milk)
- 1/2 cup vanilla ice cream (or dairy-free ice cream)
- 1/2 cup Greek yogurt (plain or vanilla)
- 1 cup crumbled jam roly-poly (store-bought or homemade, cooled; use a fruit-flavored jam)
- 1/4 cup fruit jam or preserves (such as strawberry, raspberry, or apricot)
- 1 tablespoon honey or maple syrup (optional, for extra sweetness)
- 1/4 teaspoon vanilla extract
- Ice cubes (as needed)
- Optional: Whipped cream and extra fruit jam or a sprinkle of crumbled jam roly-poly (for garnish)

Instructions:

1. **Prepare Jam Roly-Poly:** If using store-bought jam roly-poly, crumble it into small pieces. If homemade, ensure it is cooled and crumbled before adding to the blender.
2. **Blend Ingredients:** In a blender, combine the milk, vanilla ice cream, Greek yogurt, crumbled jam roly-poly, fruit jam or preserves, honey or maple syrup (if using), and vanilla extract.
3. **Add Ice:** Add a handful of ice cubes for a thicker, colder shake.
4. **Blend:** Blend on high until smooth and creamy. If the shake is too thick, add more milk to reach your desired consistency.
5. **Taste and Adjust:** Taste the shake and adjust sweetness or fruit flavor if needed by adding more honey or jam.
6. **Serve:** Pour the shake into a glass. Optionally, top with whipped cream and a drizzle of extra fruit jam or a sprinkle of crumbled jam roly-poly for added flavor and a decorative touch.

Enjoy your Fruity Jam Roly-Poly Shake! It's a creamy, fruity treat that brings the classic flavors of jam roly-poly into a refreshing and indulgent milkshake.

Nutella and Banana British Classic Shake

Ingredients:

- 1 cup milk (dairy or non-dairy, such as almond or oat milk)
- 1/2 cup vanilla ice cream (or dairy-free ice cream)
- 1/2 cup Greek yogurt (plain or vanilla)
- 2 ripe bananas (peeled and sliced)
- 1/4 cup Nutella (or other chocolate-hazelnut spread)
- 1 tablespoon honey or maple syrup (optional, for extra sweetness)
- 1/4 teaspoon vanilla extract
- Ice cubes (as needed)
- Optional: Whipped cream and a drizzle of Nutella (for garnish)

Instructions:

1. **Prepare Bananas:** Peel and slice the ripe bananas. For a creamier texture, you can freeze the banana slices before use.
2. **Blend Ingredients:** In a blender, combine the milk, vanilla ice cream, Greek yogurt, banana slices, Nutella, honey or maple syrup (if using), and vanilla extract.
3. **Add Ice:** Add a handful of ice cubes for a thicker, colder shake.
4. **Blend:** Blend on high until smooth and creamy. If the shake is too thick, add more milk to achieve your desired consistency.
5. **Taste and Adjust:** Taste the shake and adjust sweetness if needed by adding more honey or Nutella.
6. **Serve:** Pour the shake into a glass. Optionally, top with whipped cream and a drizzle of Nutella for a decorative touch.

Enjoy your Nutella and Banana British Classic Shake! It's a creamy, indulgent treat that combines the rich flavors of Nutella with the natural sweetness of bananas, perfect for a refreshing and satisfying milkshake.

Oat Biscuit Shake

Ingredients:

- 1 cup milk (dairy or non-dairy, such as almond or oat milk)
- 1/2 cup vanilla ice cream (or dairy-free ice cream)
- 1/2 cup Greek yogurt (plain or vanilla)
- 4-6 oat biscuits or oat cookies (crumbled; you can use store-bought or homemade)
- 2 tablespoons honey or maple syrup (optional, for extra sweetness)
- 1/4 teaspoon ground cinnamon (optional, for extra flavor)
- 1/4 teaspoon vanilla extract
- Ice cubes (as needed)
- Optional: Whipped cream and extra crumbled oat biscuits (for garnish)

Instructions:

1. **Prepare Oat Biscuits:** If using store-bought oat biscuits or cookies, crumble them into small pieces. You can do this using a food processor or by placing them in a sealed bag and crushing them with a rolling pin.
2. **Blend Ingredients:** In a blender, combine the milk, vanilla ice cream, Greek yogurt, crumbled oat biscuits, honey or maple syrup (if using), ground cinnamon (if using), and vanilla extract.
3. **Add Ice:** Add a handful of ice cubes for a thicker, colder shake.
4. **Blend:** Blend on high until smooth and creamy. If the shake is too thick, add more milk to achieve your desired consistency.
5. **Taste and Adjust:** Taste the shake and adjust sweetness or spice if needed by adding more honey or cinnamon.
6. **Serve:** Pour the shake into a glass. Optionally, top with whipped cream and a sprinkle of extra crumbled oat biscuits for added texture and a decorative touch.

Enjoy your Oat Biscuit Shake! It's a creamy and hearty treat that captures the comforting flavors of oat biscuits in a refreshing milkshake.

Plum and Almond Bake Shake

Ingredients:

- 1 cup milk (dairy or non-dairy, such as almond or oat milk)
- 1/2 cup vanilla ice cream (or dairy-free ice cream)
- 1/2 cup Greek yogurt (plain or vanilla)
- 1 cup fresh or frozen plums (pitted and chopped)
- 1/4 cup almond flour or ground almonds
- 1 tablespoon honey or maple syrup (optional, for extra sweetness)
- 1/4 teaspoon almond extract (optional, for enhanced almond flavor)
- Ice cubes (as needed)
- Optional: Whipped cream, toasted almonds, and extra plum slices (for garnish)

Instructions:

1. **Prepare Plums:** Wash, pit, and chop the plums into small pieces. If using frozen plums, let them thaw slightly. If you prefer a smoother texture, you can cook the plums lightly until they're soft, then cool them before using.
2. **Blend Ingredients:** In a blender, combine the milk, vanilla ice cream, Greek yogurt, chopped plums, almond flour or ground almonds, honey or maple syrup (if using), and almond extract (if using).
3. **Add Ice:** Add a handful of ice cubes for a thicker, colder shake.
4. **Blend:** Blend on high until smooth and creamy. If the shake is too thick, add more milk to achieve your desired consistency.
5. **Taste and Adjust:** Taste the shake and adjust sweetness or almond flavor if needed by adding more honey or almond extract.
6. **Serve:** Pour the shake into a glass. Optionally, top with whipped cream, a sprinkle of toasted almonds, and extra plum slices for a decorative touch.

Enjoy your Plum and Almond Bake Shake! It's a creamy, fruity, and nutty treat that combines the comforting flavors of a baked plum dessert with the richness of a milkshake.

Lemon and Poppy Seed Shake

Ingredients:

- 1 cup milk (dairy or non-dairy, such as almond or oat milk)
- 1/2 cup vanilla ice cream (or dairy-free ice cream)
- 1/2 cup Greek yogurt (plain or vanilla)
- 1/4 cup freshly squeezed lemon juice (about 1 lemon)
- 1 tablespoon lemon zest (about 1 lemon)
- 1 tablespoon poppy seeds
- 1-2 tablespoons honey or maple syrup (optional, for extra sweetness)
- 1/4 teaspoon vanilla extract (optional)
- Ice cubes (as needed)
- Optional: Whipped cream and extra lemon zest or poppy seeds (for garnish)

Instructions:

1. **Prepare Ingredients:** Zest and juice the lemon. Set aside.
2. **Blend Ingredients:** In a blender, combine the milk, vanilla ice cream, Greek yogurt, lemon juice, lemon zest, poppy seeds, and honey or maple syrup (if using). Add vanilla extract if desired.
3. **Add Ice:** Add a handful of ice cubes for a thicker, colder shake.
4. **Blend:** Blend on high until smooth and creamy. If the shake is too thick, add more milk to reach your desired consistency.
5. **Taste and Adjust:** Taste the shake and adjust sweetness or lemon flavor if needed by adding more honey or lemon juice.
6. **Serve:** Pour the shake into a glass. Optionally, top with whipped cream and a sprinkle of extra lemon zest or poppy seeds for added flavor and a decorative touch.

Enjoy your Lemon and Poppy Seed Shake! It's a bright, creamy treat that captures the refreshing flavors of lemon and the delightful crunch of poppy seeds in a refreshing milkshake.

Victoria Sponge with Strawberry Shake

Ingredients:

- 1 cup milk (dairy or non-dairy, such as almond or oat milk)
- 1/2 cup vanilla ice cream (or dairy-free ice cream)
- 1/2 cup Greek yogurt (plain or vanilla)
- 1 cup fresh strawberries (hulled; you can also use frozen strawberries)
- 2 slices of vanilla sponge cake (cut into small pieces; store-bought or homemade)
- 2 tablespoons strawberry jam (optional, for extra strawberry flavor)
- 1 tablespoon honey or maple syrup (optional, for extra sweetness)
- 1/4 teaspoon vanilla extract
- Ice cubes (as needed)
- Optional: Whipped cream and extra strawberries or cake crumbs (for garnish)

Instructions:

1. **Prepare Strawberries:** Wash and hull the fresh strawberries. If using frozen strawberries, let them thaw slightly before use.
2. **Prepare Sponge Cake:** Cut the vanilla sponge cake into small pieces. If the cake is dry, you can lightly toast it or warm it slightly to make it easier to blend.
3. **Blend Ingredients:** In a blender, combine the milk, vanilla ice cream, Greek yogurt, strawberries, sponge cake pieces, and strawberry jam (if using). Add honey or maple syrup if desired, and vanilla extract.
4. **Add Ice:** Add a handful of ice cubes for a thicker, colder shake.
5. **Blend:** Blend on high until smooth and creamy. If the shake is too thick, add more milk to reach your desired consistency.
6. **Taste and Adjust:** Taste the shake and adjust sweetness or strawberry flavor if needed by adding more honey or jam.
7. **Serve:** Pour the shake into a glass. Optionally, top with whipped cream and a sprinkle of extra strawberries or cake crumbs for a decorative touch.

Enjoy your Victoria Sponge with Strawberry Shake! It's a creamy, nostalgic treat that combines the flavors of a classic sponge cake with fresh strawberries in a refreshing milkshake.

Pecan Pie Shake

Ingredients:

- 1 cup milk (dairy or non-dairy, such as almond or oat milk)
- 1/2 cup vanilla ice cream (or dairy-free ice cream)
- 1/2 cup Greek yogurt (plain or vanilla)
- 1/2 cup chopped pecans (toasted for extra flavor)
- 1/4 cup pecan pie filling (store-bought or homemade)
- 1 tablespoon maple syrup or honey (optional, for extra sweetness)
- 1/4 teaspoon vanilla extract
- Ice cubes (as needed)
- Optional: Whipped cream, extra chopped pecans, and a drizzle of caramel sauce (for garnish)

Instructions:

1. **Prepare Pecans:** If desired, toast the pecans in a dry skillet over medium heat until fragrant and slightly golden, about 3-4 minutes. Allow them to cool before using.
2. **Blend Ingredients:** In a blender, combine the milk, vanilla ice cream, Greek yogurt, chopped pecans, pecan pie filling, and maple syrup or honey (if using). Add vanilla extract.
3. **Add Ice:** Add a handful of ice cubes for a thicker, colder shake.
4. **Blend:** Blend on high until smooth and creamy. If the shake is too thick, add more milk to achieve your desired consistency.
5. **Taste and Adjust:** Taste the shake and adjust sweetness if needed by adding more maple syrup or honey.
6. **Serve:** Pour the shake into a glass. Optionally, top with whipped cream, a sprinkle of extra chopped pecans, and a drizzle of caramel sauce for a decorative and indulgent touch.

Enjoy your Pecan Pie Shake! It's a creamy and nutty treat that brings the comforting flavors of pecan pie into a refreshing milkshake.

Blackberry and Apple Crumble Shake

Ingredients:

- 1 cup milk (dairy or non-dairy, such as almond or oat milk)
- 1/2 cup vanilla ice cream (or dairy-free ice cream)
- 1/2 cup Greek yogurt (plain or vanilla)
- 1 cup fresh or frozen blackberries
- 1 small apple (peeled, cored, and chopped)
- 1/2 cup crumble topping (store-bought or homemade; see instructions below)
- 1 tablespoon honey or maple syrup (optional, for extra sweetness)
- 1/4 teaspoon vanilla extract
- Ice cubes (as needed)
- Optional: Whipped cream and extra crumble topping for garnish

Instructions:

1. **Prepare Ingredients:**
   - If using fresh blackberries, wash them. If using frozen, let them thaw slightly.
   - Peel, core, and chop the apple into small pieces.
   - If making homemade crumble topping, mix together equal parts flour, oats, and brown sugar with a pinch of cinnamon. Cut in butter until the mixture resembles coarse crumbs, then bake at 350°F (175°C) for about 10-15 minutes until golden brown and crisp. Allow it to cool before using.
2. **Blend Ingredients:**
   - In a blender, combine the milk, vanilla ice cream, Greek yogurt, blackberries, chopped apple, and crumble topping. Add honey or maple syrup if desired, and vanilla extract.
3. **Add Ice:**
   - Add a handful of ice cubes for a thicker, colder shake.
4. **Blend:**
   - Blend on high until smooth and creamy. If the shake is too thick, add more milk to reach your desired consistency.
5. **Taste and Adjust:**
   - Taste the shake and adjust sweetness if needed by adding more honey or maple syrup.
6. **Serve:**
   - Pour the shake into a glass. Optionally, top with whipped cream and a sprinkle of extra crumble topping for added texture and a decorative touch.

Enjoy your Blackberry and Apple Crumble Shake! It's a creamy, fruity treat that brings together the delightful flavors of blackberry and apple crumble in a refreshing milkshake.

Rhubarb and Ginger Shake

Ingredients:

- 1 cup milk (dairy or non-dairy, such as almond or oat milk)
- 1/2 cup vanilla ice cream (or dairy-free ice cream)
- 1/2 cup Greek yogurt (plain or vanilla)
- 1 cup fresh or frozen rhubarb (chopped; if using fresh, cook it lightly)
- 1-2 tablespoons honey or maple syrup (optional, for extra sweetness)
- 1/2 teaspoon ground ginger (or 1 teaspoon fresh grated ginger)
- 1/4 teaspoon vanilla extract
- Ice cubes (as needed)
- Optional: Whipped cream and a sprinkle of chopped crystallized ginger (for garnish)

Instructions:

1. **Prepare Rhubarb:**
   - If using fresh rhubarb, chop it into small pieces and cook it in a saucepan with a little water until tender, about 5-7 minutes. Allow it to cool before using. If using frozen rhubarb, let it thaw slightly.
2. **Blend Ingredients:**
   - In a blender, combine the milk, vanilla ice cream, Greek yogurt, cooked or thawed rhubarb, honey or maple syrup (if using), ground ginger or fresh grated ginger, and vanilla extract.
3. **Add Ice:**
   - Add a handful of ice cubes for a thicker, colder shake.
4. **Blend:**
   - Blend on high until smooth and creamy. If the shake is too thick, add more milk to reach your desired consistency.
5. **Taste and Adjust:**
   - Taste the shake and adjust sweetness or ginger flavor if needed by adding more honey or ginger.
6. **Serve:**
   - Pour the shake into a glass. Optionally, top with whipped cream and a sprinkle of chopped crystallized ginger for added flavor and a decorative touch.

Enjoy your Rhubarb and Ginger Shake! It's a creamy and refreshing treat that combines the tangy taste of rhubarb with the warming spice of ginger for a unique and flavorful milkshake.

Chocolate Marshmallow Shake

Ingredients:

- 1 cup milk (dairy or non-dairy, such as almond or oat milk)
- 1/2 cup chocolate ice cream (or dairy-free chocolate ice cream)
- 1/2 cup Greek yogurt (plain or vanilla)
- 1/4 cup mini marshmallows (plus extra for garnish)
- 1/4 cup chocolate syrup or hot fudge sauce
- 1 tablespoon cocoa powder (optional, for extra chocolate flavor)
- 1/4 teaspoon vanilla extract
- Ice cubes (as needed)
- Optional: Whipped cream, extra marshmallows, and chocolate shavings (for garnish)

Instructions:

1. **Blend Ingredients:**
    - In a blender, combine the milk, chocolate ice cream, Greek yogurt, mini marshmallows, chocolate syrup or hot fudge sauce, and cocoa powder (if using). Add vanilla extract.
2. **Add Ice:**
    - Add a handful of ice cubes for a thicker, colder shake.
3. **Blend:**
    - Blend on high until smooth and creamy. If the shake is too thick, add more milk to achieve your desired consistency.
4. **Taste and Adjust:**
    - Taste the shake and adjust sweetness or chocolate flavor if needed by adding more chocolate syrup or marshmallows.
5. **Serve:**
    - Pour the shake into a glass. Optionally, top with whipped cream, extra marshmallows, and chocolate shavings for a decorative and indulgent touch.

Enjoy your Chocolate Marshmallow Shake! It's a rich, creamy treat that combines the delightful flavors of chocolate and marshmallows in a refreshing milkshake.

Peach Melba Shake

Ingredients:

- 1 cup milk (dairy or non-dairy, such as almond or oat milk)
- 1/2 cup vanilla ice cream (or dairy-free vanilla ice cream)
- 1/2 cup Greek yogurt (plain or vanilla)
- 1 cup fresh or frozen peaches (peeled, pitted, and chopped)
- 1/4 cup raspberry puree or raspberry jam (store-bought or homemade)
- 1 tablespoon honey or maple syrup (optional, for extra sweetness)
- 1/4 teaspoon vanilla extract
- Ice cubes (as needed)
- Optional: Whipped cream and fresh peach slices or raspberry for garnish

Instructions:

1. **Prepare Peaches:**
   - If using fresh peaches, peel, pit, and chop them into small pieces. If using frozen peaches, let them thaw slightly. You can also lightly cook fresh peaches with a bit of honey to enhance their flavor, then let them cool before using.
2. **Prepare Raspberry Puree:**
   - If making homemade raspberry puree, blend fresh or thawed raspberries until smooth. You can strain it to remove seeds if desired. Alternatively, use store-bought raspberry jam for convenience.
3. **Blend Ingredients:**
   - In a blender, combine the milk, vanilla ice cream, Greek yogurt, peaches, raspberry puree or jam, and honey or maple syrup (if using). Add vanilla extract.
4. **Add Ice:**
   - Add a handful of ice cubes for a thicker, colder shake.
5. **Blend:**
   - Blend on high until smooth and creamy. If the shake is too thick, add more milk to achieve your desired consistency.
6. **Taste and Adjust:**
   - Taste the shake and adjust sweetness if needed by adding more honey or raspberry puree.
7. **Serve:**
   - Pour the shake into a glass. Optionally, top with whipped cream and garnish with fresh peach slices or raspberries for a decorative touch.

Enjoy your Peach Melba Shake! It's a creamy, fruity treat that captures the essence of the classic Peach Melba dessert in a refreshing and indulgent milkshake.

Traditional English Trifle Shake

Ingredients:

- 1 cup milk (dairy or non-dairy, such as almond or oat milk)
- 1/2 cup vanilla ice cream (or dairy-free vanilla ice cream)
- 1/2 cup Greek yogurt (plain or vanilla)
- 1/2 cup fresh or frozen berries (e.g., strawberries, raspberries, or a mixed berry blend)
- 1/2 cup sponge cake or ladyfingers (cut into small pieces; store-bought or homemade)
- 1/4 cup custard (store-bought or homemade; if you prefer a lighter texture, use Greek yogurt)
- 1 tablespoon honey or maple syrup (optional, for extra sweetness)
- 1/4 teaspoon vanilla extract
- Ice cubes (as needed)
- Optional: Whipped cream, extra berries, and crumbled sponge cake or ladyfingers (for garnish)

Instructions:

1. **Prepare Berries:**
   - If using fresh berries, wash them. If using frozen, let them thaw slightly. You can also blend the berries into a puree for a smoother texture if desired.
2. **Prepare Sponge Cake or Ladyfingers:**
   - Cut the sponge cake or ladyfingers into small pieces. If they are dry, lightly toast them or warm them slightly to make them easier to blend.
3. **Blend Ingredients:**
   - In a blender, combine the milk, vanilla ice cream, Greek yogurt, berries, sponge cake or ladyfingers, custard, and honey or maple syrup (if using). Add vanilla extract.
4. **Add Ice:**
   - Add a handful of ice cubes for a thicker, colder shake.
5. **Blend:**
   - Blend on high until smooth and creamy. If the shake is too thick, add more milk to achieve your desired consistency.
6. **Taste and Adjust:**
   - Taste the shake and adjust sweetness or berry flavor if needed by adding more honey or berries.
7. **Serve:**
   - Pour the shake into a glass. Optionally, top with whipped cream and garnish with extra berries and crumbled sponge cake or ladyfingers for a decorative and indulgent touch.

Enjoy your Traditional English Trifle Shake! It's a creamy, fruity treat that brings together the classic layers of a traditional trifle into a refreshing and delicious milkshake.

Sticky Date and Walnut Shake

Ingredients:

- 1 cup milk (dairy or non-dairy, such as almond or oat milk)
- 1/2 cup vanilla ice cream (or dairy-free vanilla ice cream)
- 1/2 cup Greek yogurt (plain or vanilla)
- 1/2 cup pitted dates (chopped; you can soak them in warm water for a few minutes if they're dry)
- 1/4 cup chopped walnuts (toasted for extra flavor, if desired)
- 2 tablespoons caramel sauce or toffee sauce (store-bought or homemade)
- 1 tablespoon honey or maple syrup (optional, for extra sweetness)
- 1/4 teaspoon vanilla extract
- Ice cubes (as needed)
- Optional: Whipped cream and extra chopped walnuts for garnish

Instructions:

1. **Prepare Dates:**
   - If the dates are dry, soak them in warm water for 10-15 minutes to soften. Drain before using. Chop the dates into small pieces.
2. **Prepare Walnuts:**
   - If desired, toast the chopped walnuts in a dry skillet over medium heat until fragrant and slightly golden, about 3-4 minutes. Allow them to cool before using.
3. **Blend Ingredients:**
   - In a blender, combine the milk, vanilla ice cream, Greek yogurt, chopped dates, toasted walnuts, caramel sauce or toffee sauce, and honey or maple syrup (if using). Add vanilla extract.
4. **Add Ice:**
   - Add a handful of ice cubes for a thicker, colder shake.
5. **Blend:**
   - Blend on high until smooth and creamy. If the shake is too thick, add more milk to achieve your desired consistency.
6. **Taste and Adjust:**
   - Taste the shake and adjust sweetness or flavor if needed by adding more honey or caramel sauce.
7. **Serve:**
   - Pour the shake into a glass. Optionally, top with whipped cream and a sprinkle of extra chopped walnuts for a decorative and indulgent touch.

Enjoy your Sticky Date and Walnut Shake! It's a creamy and indulgent treat that brings together the rich flavors of sticky toffee pudding with the crunch of walnuts in a refreshing milkshake.

www.ingramcontent.com/pod-product-compliance
Lightning Source LLC
LaVergne TN
LVHW081506060526
838201LV00056BA/2971